Healthy Kitchen®

Cook!

Imprint

WW Publishing Team
Samantha Rees, Nicola Hill,
Ruby Bamford, Nicola Kirk

For Seven Publishing Ltd
Food
Food editor: Nadine Brown
Recipes: Cate Dixon, Jenna Leiter

Editorial
Editor-in-Chief: Helen Renshaw
Editor: Ward Hellewell
Sub-editors: Julie Stevens,
Christine Faughlin, Sarah Nittinger

Design & photography
Art director: Liz Baird
Photographer: Ant Duncan
Food stylists: Sarah Cook, Emily Kydd
Prop stylist: Tonia Shuttleworth

Account management
Account manager: Gina Cavaciuti
Group publishing director: Kirsten Price

Production
Senior production manager: Liz Knipe
Colour reproduction by F1 Colour
Printed in the UK by CPI Colour

Seven ⒸⓏ

Produced by Seven Publishing on behalf of WW International, Inc.
Published March 2019. All rights reserved. No part of this
publication may be reproduced, stored in a retrieval system
or transmitted in any form by any means, electronic, mechanical
photocopying, recording or otherwise, without the prior written
permission of Seven Publishing. First published in Great Britain
by Seven Publishing Ltd.

Seven Publishing Ltd, 3-7 Herbal Hill, London EC1R 5EJ
www.seven.co.uk

A CIP catalogue record for this book is available from the
British Library.

ISBN: 978-1-9996673-3-7

The small print

Eggs We use medium eggs, unless otherwise stated. Pregnant women, the elderly and children should avoid recipes with eggs which are raw or not fully cooked if not produced under the British Lion code of practice.

Fruit and vegetables Recipes use medium-size fruit and veg, unless otherwise stated.

Reduced-fat soft cheese Where a recipe uses reduced-fat soft cheese, we mean a soft cheese with 30% less fat than its full-fat equivalent.

Low-fat spread When a recipe uses a low-fat spread, we mean a spread with a fat content of no more than 39%.

Microwaves If we have used a microwave in any of our recipes, the timings will be for an 850-watt microwave oven.

Prep and cook times These are approximate and meant to be guidelines only. Prep time includes all steps up to and following the main cooking time(s). Stated cook times may vary according to your oven.

Vegetarian Recipes displaying a vegetarian symbol include non-animal-based ingredients, but may also contain processed products that aren't always vegetarian, such as pesto. If you're a vegetarian, you should ensure you use vegetarian varieties and check the ingredients labels. Where we reference vegetarian Italian-style hard cheese in vegetarian recipes, we mean a cheese similar to Parmesan (which is not vegetarian) but which is suitable for vegetarians.

Vegan Recipes displaying a vegan symbol include no products made from or with the aid of animals or animal products.

Gluten free Recipes labelled as gluten free include ingredients that naturally do not contain gluten, but may also contain processed products, such as sauces, stock cubes and spice mixes. If so, you should ensure that those products do not include any gluten-containing ingredients (wheat, barley or rye) – these will be highlighted in the ingredients list on the product label. Manufacturers may also indicate whether there is a chance their product may have been accidentally contaminated with gluten during the manufacturing process. For more information and guidance on gluten-free products, visit www.coeliac.org.uk

Nut free Recipes displaying a nut free symbol include ingredients that do not contain nuts, but may include ingredients produced in facilities that also handle nut products. If you have a nut allergy, check ingredients labels for more information.

Dairy free Recipes displaying a dairy free symbol include ingredients that naturally do not contain dairy, but may include ingredients produced in facilities that also handle dairy products. If you have a dairy allergy, check ingredients labels for more information.

SmartPoints® have been calculated using the values for generic foods, not brands (except where stated). Tracking using branded items may affect the recorded SmartPoints.

When you see these symbols:

4 Tells you the SmartPoints value per serving

 Indicates a recipe is gluten free

 Indicates a recipe is vegetarian

 Indicates a recipe is vegan

 Indicates a recipe is nut free

 Indicates a recipe is dairy free

Contents

We all want to cook meals that are fuss-free and uncomplicated, especially on busy midweek evenings. With that in mind, the WW Kitchen Team has been creating recipes with simplicity at their heart to bring you this collection of 46 great-tasting meal ideas. These delicious recipes use no more than five main ingredients, plus a few storecupboard essentials such as seasonings, spices and cooking oil, which makes it easy for you to whip up tasty meals with minimum hassle. With fish and seafood, chicken and turkey, meat and veggie ideas, there's plenty to please everyone. And we've worked out the SmartPoints for every recipe, so you can easily fit them into your plan. Enjoy!

Storecupboard essentials

Keeping a well-stocked storecupboard means you can transform just a few simple ingredients into tasty meals quickly and easily. Here's a list of the storecupboard ingredients used in this book – you'll be able to use these in multiple recipes, so they're a good investment. Most have a long shelf life, but you should regularly check the best-before dates as some storecupboard ingredients – such as spices and herbs – can lose their flavour over time. We've included fresh garlic as it's used in so many recipes, but you could also use dried garlic granules, or ready-to-use prepared garlic from a jar.

DRIED HERBS & SPICES
Mixed herbs
Fennel seeds
Cumin seeds
Bay leaves
Paprika
Chilli flakes
Ground cumin
Ground coriander
Curry powder
Dried thyme
Za'atar

FLAVOURINGS
Fresh garlic
Stock cubes
(vegetable, fish,
chicken, beef
and lamb)
Mustard (Dijon)

OILS
Calorie controlled
cooking spray
Vegetable
Sunflower
Olive

SAUCES
Ketchup
Soy sauce

SEASONING
Salt (sea
salt and
table salt)
Black
peppercorns

SWEETENERS
Clear honey
Caster sugar

VINEGAR
Cider
Balsamic
White wine
Red wine

Chicken & turkey

Pesto chicken soup

serves 4   prep time 10 minutes   cook time 30 minutes

Ready-made pesto adds plenty of flavour to this simple soup.

2 x 400g tins cannellini beans, drained and rinsed

400g cooked skinless chicken breast fillets, coarsely shredded

200g young leaf spinach

1½ tablespoons reduced-fat green pesto

20g Parmesan shavings

FROM THE STORECUPBOARD

2 chicken stock cubes

1 teaspoon chilli flakes

2 bay leaves

1 Put the beans, chicken, stock cubes, chilli flakes and bay leaves in a large deep pan. Add enough water to cover all the ingredients (about 1 litre) and bring to the boil.

2 Reduce to a simmer and cook for 30 minutes, stirring occasionally. Remove and discard the bay leaves, then lightly crush the beans with a potato masher.

3 Add the spinach and allow to wilt, then take the pan off the heat. Swirl through the pesto and season to taste.

4 Divide the soup between bowls and serve topped with the Parmesan shavings.

2   **SmartPoints value per serving**

Cook's tip

You could use other types of tinned beans in this recipe – butter beans or haricot beans also work well.

Curried chicken & sweet potato traybake

serves 4   **prep time 15 minutes + marinating**   **cook time 45 minutes**

An easy, all-in-one traybake with lightly spiced chicken and sweet potatoes.

100g 0% fat natural Greek yogurt

4 x 165g skinless chicken breast fillets

600g sweet potatoes, scrubbed and cut into wedges

400g tin chickpeas, drained and rinsed

1 lemon, sliced

FROM THE STORECUPBOARD

1½ tablespoons mild curry powder

2 garlic cloves, chopped

1 tablespoon extra-virgin olive oil

TO SERVE (optional)
Rocket

1   In a large bowl, mix together the yogurt, 1 tablespoon of the curry powder and the garlic, then season well. Add the chicken and turn to coat. Cover and marinate in the fridge for at least 2 hours or preferably overnight.

2   Preheat the oven to 200°C, fan 180°C, gas mark 6. Put the sweet potatoes, chickpeas and lemon in a baking tray, add the oil and remaining curry powder, then season to taste. Toss everything together, then arrange in a single layer. Top with the chicken and roast for 40-45 minutes until the chicken is cooked through and the sweet potato is tender, then serve.

  SmartPoints value per serving

Cook's tip
Scrub the sweet potatoes under cold running water with a clean scrubbing brush before cutting them into wedges – there's no need to peel them.

Breaded lemon turkey steaks

serves 4   **prep time** 20 minutes + marinating   **cook time** 40 minutes

These crumbed turkey steaks are served with crushed parsley potatoes.

Grated zest and juice of 1 lemon, plus lemon wedges, to serve

4 x 150g turkey steaks

600g new potatoes

Small handful fresh flat-leaf parsley, finely chopped

50g fresh breadcrumbs

FROM THE STORECUPBOARD

1 teaspoon dried mixed herbs

2 tablespoons olive oil

TO SERVE (optional)

Mixed salad leaves

1   In a non-metallic bowl, mix together the lemon zest and juice and the mixed herbs. Season to taste, then add the turkey steaks and toss together to coat. Cover and marinate in the fridge for at least 2 hours or overnight.

2   Cook the potatoes in a large pan of simmering water, for 35-40 minutes until tender. Drain and steam dry for 2 minutes, then crush lightly with the back of a fork and stir through the parsley.

3   Meanwhile, put the breadcrumbs on a plate. Add the turkey steaks, one at a time, pressing them into the breadcrumbs to coat on both sides.

4   Heat half the oil in a large nonstick frying pan and add 2 of the steaks. Cook for 4-5 minutes on each side until cooked through. Transfer to a plate lined with kitchen paper and keep warm. Heat the remaining oil in the pan and cook the remaining turkey steaks. Serve the turkey and potatoes with the lemon wedges.

 SmartPoints value per serving

Cook's tip

You could also use chicken breast fillets in this recipe for no extra SmartPoints. Flatten them between 2 pieces of clingfilm before crumbing.

Sticky peanut butter chicken

serves 4   prep time 15 minutes   cook time 15 minutes

A simple take on satay chicken, with lime juice adding a zesty tang.

200g basmati rice

4 x 165g skinless chicken breast fillets, cut into strips

25g PBFit peanut butter powder, dissolved in 40ml boiling water

Grated zest and juice of 1 lime, plus lime wedges, to serve

4 spring onions, trimmed and thinly sliced

FROM THE STORECUPBOARD
Calorie controlled cooking spray
1 teaspoon mild curry powder
1 teaspoon chilli flakes
2 tablespoons clear honey
1 tablespoon soy sauce

TO SERVE (optional)
Fresh coriander leaves

1   Cook the rice to pack instructions.

2   Meanwhile, set a nonstick frying pan over a medium heat and mist with cooking spray. Sprinkle the chicken strips with the curry powder and chilli flakes, then cook for 8-10 minutes, turning occasionally, until golden and cooked through.

3   In a small bowl, combine the PBFit mixture, honey and soy sauce with 2 tablespoons water, then add to the pan. Stir to combine and cook for a further 2 minutes.

4   Remove from the heat, then add the lime zest and juice and most of the spring onions. Season to taste and stir to combine.

5   Fluff up the rice with a fork and divide between bowls, then top with the sticky chicken. Top with the remaining spring onions and serve with the lime wedges.

 SmartPoints value per serving

Cook's tip
To make this gluten free, use 1 tablespoon tamari instead of soy sauce, for no extra SmartPoints.

Chicken & leek risotto

serves 4   prep time 15 minutes   cook time 35 minutes   freezable

A delicious risotto that you can batch cook and freeze for later.

2 leeks, trimmed and finely sliced

2 x 165g skinless chicken breast fillets, cut into 2cm pieces

300g risotto rice

50g frozen peas

40g Parmesan, finely grated

FROM THE STORECUPBOARD
Calorie controlled cooking spray
1 garlic clove, thinly sliced
1 teaspoon dried thyme
1 litre chicken stock, made with 2 stock cubes

1 Set a deep, lidded nonstick frying pan over a medium-low heat and mist with cooking spray. Add the leeks, then cover and cook for 5 minutes, stirring once, until softened – you may need to add a splash of water if they start to stick. Add the garlic and cook for a further 1 minute.

2 Add the chicken pieces and thyme to the pan and cook, uncovered, for 5 minutes until the chicken is lightly golden.

3 Add the rice to the pan, stir to combine, then cook for 2 minutes. Gradually add the stock, a ladleful at a time, stirring until it has been absorbed. Continue cooking until the rice is tender but still retains a little bite and has a glossy sauce surrounding it; this should take about 20 minutes. Add the peas for the final 2 minutes of the cooking time.

4 Remove from the heat and stir through half the Parmesan. Serve topped with the remaining Parmesan and some freshly ground black pepper.

The risotto can be frozen in an airtight container for up to 2 months.

  SmartPoints value per serving

Cook's tip
The risotto should be stirred constantly during cooking – as well as stopping it from sticking to the pan, this helps release the starch in the rice to give the risotto its creamy texture.

Chicken tikka & pickled onion pizzas

serves 4   prep time 15 minutes + pickling & resting   cook time 30 minutes

Fragrant, lightly pickled onion makes these easy pizzas deliciously different.

1 red onion, thinly sliced

3 x 165g skinless chicken breast fillets

2½ tablespoons tikka curry paste

2½ tablespoons 0% fat natural Greek yogurt

4 mini naan breads

FROM THE STORECUPBOARD
Calorie controlled cooking spray
1 teaspoon cumin seeds
3 tablespoons red wine vinegar
1 tablespoon caster sugar

TO SERVE (optional)
Fresh coriander leaves

1 Heat the grill to medium and mist a baking tray with cooking spray.

2 Toast the cumin seeds in a pan over a medium heat until they release their aroma. Remove from the heat and set aside.

3 Mix the red onion and half the toasted cumin seeds together in a non-metallic bowl. Heat the vinegar, sugar and a pinch of salt in a small pan over a medium heat and simmer until the sugar has dissolved. Pour the vinegar mixture over the red onion and cumin seeds and stir to combine. Leave to pickle for 30 minutes.

4 Meanwhile, in a bowl, coat the chicken with 2 tablespoons of the tikka paste and place on the prepared baking tray. Mist with cooking spray and grill for 20 minutes, turning halfway, until cooked through. Leave to rest for 10 minutes, then cut into strips. In a bowl, combine the yogurt and remaining tikka paste, then set aside.

5 Put the naan breads under the grill for 2 minutes to heat through, then top each with the chicken and pickled onion. Drizzle over the tikka yogurt, scatter over the remaining cumin seeds and serve.

 7 SmartPoints value per serving

Cook's tip
For a more intense cumin flavour, lightly crush the seeds with a pestle and mortar after toasting them in the pan.

Turkey meatloaf

serves 4   prep time 20 minutes + cooling   cook time 55 minutes   freezable

A family favourite, this uses ZeroPoint turkey mince to keep the SmartPoints low.

2 red onions, finely chopped
500g turkey breast mince
80g fresh breadcrumbs
1 egg, beaten
400g prepared butternut squash, cut into chunks

FROM THE STORECUPBOARD
Calorie controlled cooking spray
2 teaspoons dried mixed herbs
1 teaspoon chilli flakes
2 garlic cloves, finely chopped
75g tomato ketchup

1   Preheat the oven to 180°C, fan 160°C, gas mark 4. Grease a 450g loaf tin with calorie controlled cooking spray, then line with baking paper.

2   Put a small pan over a medium heat and mist with cooking spray. Fry the onions, mixed herbs and chilli flakes for 6-8 minutes, stirring occasionally, until the onions have softened – add a splash of water if they start to stick. Add the garlic and cook for a further 1 minute. Set aside to cool slightly.

3   Put the cooled onion mixture in a large bowl with the turkey mince, breadcrumbs and egg. Mix with a wooden spoon until well combined. Season to taste, then spoon into the prepared loaf tin, pushing the mixture right into the corners.

4   Put the loaf tin in a deep roasting tray and pour enough just-boiled water from the kettle to come halfway up the sides of the loaf tin. Bake for 30-35 minutes until the meatloaf starts to shrink away from the sides of the tin. Cool in the tin for 10 minutes, then turn out of the tin onto a baking tray and spread the ketchup over the top and sides of the meatloaf. Return to the oven for a further 10 minutes.

5   Meanwhile, bring a large pan of water to the boil. Add the butternut squash and cook for 15-20 minutes or until tender. Drain, then mash and season to taste. Slice the meatloaf and serve with the butternut squash mash.

The meatloaf can be frozen in an airtight container for up to 2 months.

Cook's tip
If you're freezing the meatloaf, cut it into portions first to make thawing and reheating quicker and easier.

3   SmartPoints value per serving

Fennel grilled chicken with apple & potato salad

serves 4 **prep time** 15 minutes + resting **cook time** 35 minutes

Potato salad with a fruity twist is served with tender griddled chicken fillets.

800g new potatoes, halved or quartered if large

4 x 165g skinless chicken breast fillets

5 tablespoons 0% fat natural Greek yogurt

2 Braeburn apples, cored and cut into matchsticks

1 red onion, thinly sliced

FROM THE STORECUPBOARD

1 tablespoon fennel seeds

Calorie controlled cooking spray

1 tablespoon white wine vinegar

1 teaspoon Dijon mustard

TO SERVE (optional)
Rocket

1 Put the potatoes in a pan of cold water. Bring to the boil, then simmer for 20-25 minutes or until tender. Drain and leave to cool in a colander.

2 Meanwhile, put the chicken breasts between 2 sheets of baking paper and bash with a rolling pin to tenderise – you'll need to do this in batches.

3 Mix together the fennel seeds and some seasoning, then sprinkle over both sides of the chicken. Mist with cooking spray.

4 Heat a nonstick griddle or frying pan over a high heat and fry the chicken breasts for 6-8 minutes on each side until cooked through. Transfer the chicken to a warm plate, cover with kitchen foil and leave to rest for 10 minutes, then cut into slices.

5 In a large bowl, whisk together the yogurt, vinegar and mustard, and season to taste. Add the potatoes, apples and onion to the dressing and toss gently to coat. Divide between plates and serve with the chicken.

 SmartPoints value per serving

Cook's tip
Instead of fennel seeds, try using a mixture of 1½ teaspoons each of cumin and coriander seeds, for no extra SmartPoints.

Chicken sausage & cherry tomato pasta

serves 4   prep time 15 minutes   cook time 40 minutes

This no-fuss, flavoursome pasta dish makes a great choice for a family meal.

1 red onion, thinly sliced
340g pack chicken chipolata sausages (we used Heck Italia)
100g medium-fat soft cheese
200g cherry tomatoes, quartered
240g fusilli pasta

FROM THE STORECUPBOARD
2 teaspoons fennel seeds
Calorie controlled cooking spray
2 garlic cloves, finely chopped
1 teaspoon chilli flakes
350ml chicken stock, made with 1 stock cube

TO SERVE (optional)
Fresh basil leaves

1 Heat a nonstick frying pan over a medium heat. Add the fennel seeds and toast for 1-2 minutes until they release their aroma. Remove from the pan and finely grind in a spice grinder or using a pestle and mortar. Set aside.

2 Mist the pan with cooking spray and add the onion. Cook for 6-8 minutes until softened. Add the garlic and cook for a further 1 minute.

3 Squeeze the sausage meat out of the casings and into the pan and break up with a wooden spoon. Add the ground fennel seeds and chilli flakes, then cook for 8 minutes until the meat is golden. Pour in the stock and simmer for 20 minutes until the sauce is thick. Remove from the heat and stir through the soft cheese and tomatoes.

4 Meanwhile, cook the pasta to pack instructions.

5 Drain the pasta well and add it to the pan with the sausage mixture. Stir to combine and season to taste, then serve.

 9   **SmartPoints value per serving**

Cook's tip
Use wholemeal pasta instead of white, if you prefer, for no extra SmartPoints.

Slow-cooked balsamic chicken

serves 4   prep time 15 minutes + resting   cook time 1 hour 5 minutes

An easy, Italian-inspired pasta dish that makes a great weekend dinner.

4 x 165g skinless chicken breast fillets
200g cherry tomatoes, halved
15g fresh basil, leaves picked, half torn, the rest left whole
200g spaghetti

FROM THE STORECUPBOARD
Calorie controlled cooking spray
4 garlic cloves, thinly sliced
3 tablespoons balsamic vinegar
1 teaspoon caster sugar
1 teaspoon dried thyme
1 teaspoon dried chilli flakes

1 Preheat the oven to 170°C, fan 150°C, gas mark 3. Put a nonstick frying or griddle pan over a high heat and mist with cooking spray. Fry the chicken breasts for 2 minutes on each side until lightly golden.

2 Put the garlic, tomatoes, torn basil leaves, balsamic vinegar, caster sugar, thyme and chilli flakes in a baking dish. Stir to combine, then add the chicken and season to taste.

3 Cover the dish with kitchen foil and bake for 1 hour, basting the chicken halfway, until it is cooked through. Remove the foil for the final 10 minutes of cooking time. Set aside to rest for 10 minutes.

4 Meanwhile, cook the spaghetti to pack instructions. Drain and divide between serving plates, then arrange the chicken on top with the tomatoes and garlic, and drizzle over any cooking juices from the baking dish. Garnish with the whole basil leaves, then serve.

  SmartPoints value per serving

Cook's tip
You can also cook the chicken and tomatoes in a slow cooker if you have one – cook on medium for 4 hours.

Frying pan chicken pie

serves 6   prep time 20 minutes   cook time 1 hour   freezable

This clever one-pan pie tastes amazing – and will save you time on washing-up!

8 shallots, halved

4 x 165g skinless chicken breast fillets, cut into 3cm chunks

250g chestnut mushrooms, sliced

2 tablespoons half-fat crème fraîche

375g pack ready-rolled light puff pastry (195g used)

FROM THE STORECUPBOARD

Calorie controlled cooking spray

1 garlic clove, finely chopped

1½ teaspoons dried mixed herbs

3 tablespoons plain flour

300ml chicken stock, made with 1 stock cube

TO SERVE (optional)

Steamed sugar snap peas

1   Preheat the oven to 190°C, fan 170°C, gas mark 5. Put a medium nonstick ovenproof frying pan or casserole (about 20cm in diameter) over a medium heat and mist with cooking spray. Add the shallots and garlic, and fry for 2-3 minutes until just starting to brown.

2   Increase the heat and add the chicken, mushrooms and mixed herbs to the pan and cook for 8-10 minutes until golden.

3   Reduce the heat, sprinkle over the flour and stir to combine. Gradually stir in the stock, then simmer for 3-5 minutes until thickened.

4   Take the pan off the heat, stir through the crème fraîche and season to taste. Cool slightly, then cover with the puff pastry sheet, trimming off and discarding the excess pastry.

5   Make a small hole in the middle of the pie for steam to escape, then bake for 30-40 minutes until risen and golden, then serve.

The pie filling can be frozen in an airtight container for up to 2 months.

 6   SmartPoints value per serving

Cook's tip

To make peeling the shallots easier, put them in a colander and pour over a kettle of boiling water to loosen their skins.

Fish & seafood

Baked piri piri cod

serves 4   prep time 20 minutes   cook time 55 minutes

A super-simple all-in-one dish with tender spicy cod and lots of colourful veg.

**600g sweet potatoes, scrubbed
and cut into thin wedges**
2 red onions, cut into wedges
**2 pointed red peppers, deseeded
and cut into wedges**
4 x 140g skinless cod loin fillets
**2 x 25g sachets WW Spicy
Piri Piri Sauce**

FROM THE STORECUPBOARD
1 teaspoon ground cumin
1 teaspoon paprika
1 teaspoon dried thyme
1 tablespoon extra-virgin olive oil

TO SERVE (optional)
Chopped fresh flat-leaf parsley

1   Preheat the oven to 200°C, fan 180°C, gas mark 6.

2   Put the sweet potato, onions and peppers on a large baking tray. Add the cumin, paprika, thyme and olive oil, season to taste and gently toss everything together to coat. Roast for 40 minutes until the sweet potato is just tender.

3   Put the cod on a small plate and pour over the Spicy Piri Piri Sauce, then toss gently to coat the fish. Arrange the cod on top of the vegetables and roast for a further 10-12 minutes until the fish is cooked through, then serve.

 **SmartPoints value per serving**

Cook's tip
To check the fish is cooked through, break off a small piece from one of the loins with a fork. The flesh should easily break into flakes and be opaque all the way through.

Easy fish stew

serves 4   prep time 10 minutes   cook time 35 minutes

This wonderfully rich-tasting fish stew is great for sharing with friends.

2 red onions, thinly sliced
400g tin chopped tomatoes
300g fish pie mix
100g young leaf spinach

FROM THE STORECUPBOARD
Calorie controlled cooking spray
2 garlic cloves, thinly sliced
1 teaspoon chilli flakes
2 teaspoons dried mixed herbs
200ml fish stock, made with
1 stock cube

TO SERVE (optional)
Crusty brown bread rolls

1   Set a large nonstick pan over a medium heat and mist with cooking spray. Fry the onions for 10 minutes until softened and starting to caramelise – add a splash of water if they start to stick to the pan. Add the garlic and cook for a further 1 minute.

2   Add the chopped tomatoes, chilli flakes, dried mixed herbs and stock to the pan. Bring to the boil, then simmer for 20 minutes.

3   Add the fish pie mix and spinach to the pan and stir gently to coat in the sauce. Season to taste. Gently simmer for 5 minutes until the fish is cooked through and just starting to flake and the spinach has wilted, then serve.

 SmartPoints value per serving

Cook's tip
You could serve this with 150g boiled new potatoes per person for 4 SmartPoints per serving.

Roast salmon with peas, potatoes & chorizo

serves 4   prep time 15 minutes   cook time 1 hour 10 minutes

Chorizo adds plenty of smoky, spicy flavour to this simple one-pan recipe.

600g new potatoes
150g chorizo, finely chopped
3 red onions, cut into wedges
150g frozen peas
4 x 120g skinless salmon fillets

FROM THE STORECUPBOARD
1 teaspoon dried mixed herbs
1 teaspoon paprika
1 tablespoon extra-virgin olive oil
Calorie controlled cooking spray
Freshly ground black pepper

1 Put the potatoes in a pan of cold water. Bring to the boil and simmer for 30-35 minutes until cooked. Drain and steam dry for 2 minutes, then halve.

2 Preheat the oven to 200°C, fan 180°C, gas mark 6. Toss the potatoes, chorizo, onions, dried mixed herbs, paprika and olive oil together in a roasting tray. Season to taste and roast for 20 minutes until starting to crisp up, tossing halfway through.

3 Scatter over the peas, top with the salmon fillets and season to taste. Mist with cooking spray and roast for a further 12-15 minutes until the fish is cooked through and flakes easily.

4 Grind over some fresh black pepper, then divide between plates and serve.

  SmartPoints value per serving

Cook's tip
Want to reduce the SmartPoints? Swap the new potatoes for bite-size cauliflower florets, for 6 SmartPoints per serving. There's no need to boil them first – just add them with the other ingredients in step 2.

One-pan pesto cod & rice

serves 4   prep time 10 minutes   cook time 30 minutes

A simple, all-in-one fish and rice dish that's great for midweek dinners.

200g brown basmati rice
1 large courgette, coarsely grated
2 tablespoons reduced-fat green pesto
4 x 140g skinless cod loin fillets
12 cherry tomatoes

FROM THE STORECUPBOARD
400ml vegetable stock, made with 1 stock cube
Calorie controlled cooking spray

1   Preheat the oven to 200°C, fan 180°C, gas mark 6.

2   Put the rice and stock in a 1.5-litre flameproof casserole, bring to the boil then simmer, covered, for 12 minutes, until the rice is tender and all the liquid has been absorbed. Fluff up the grains with a fork, then stir through the courgette.

3   Spread the pesto over the fish, then arrange on top of the rice with the tomatoes. Mist with cooking spray and bake, uncovered, for 12-15 minutes, until the fish is cooked through and the tomatoes are tender. Season to taste and serve.

 SmartPoints value per serving

Cook's tip
This dish would work just as well with any other firm white fish fillets, or even salmon fillets.

Smoked mackerel, spinach & new potato frittata

serves 4   prep time 15 minutes   cook time 1 hour 10 minutes

Serve slices of this tasty frittata for lunch, or pack it up for a picnic.

400g new potatoes, cut into 2mm slices

10 eggs, beaten

4 x 75g peppered smoked mackerel fillets, skin removed and fish flaked

50g young leaf spinach

30g fresh basil, leaves picked and torn

FROM THE STORECUPBOARD
1 teaspoon dried mixed herbs
1 teaspoon chilli flakes

TO SERVE (optional)
Mixed salad leaves

1 Put the potatoes in a pan of boiling water. Simmer for 8-10 minutes until tender. Drain and set aside for 2 minutes to steam dry in the pan.

2 Preheat the oven to 170°C, fan 150°C, gas mark 3. Line a 23cm x 12cm x 5cm deep rectangular baking dish with baking paper.

3 In a large bowl, whisk together the eggs, dried mixed herbs, chilli flakes and 1 tablespoon water and season to taste.

4 Layer the potatoes, mackerel, spinach and basil in the prepared baking dish. Pour over the egg mixture and bake for 50 minutes to 1 hour until the egg is cooked through. Slice and serve.

8 SmartPoints value per serving

Cook's tip

Take care not to overcook the frittata or the eggs will become tough. You can serve this straight from the oven, but it's just as good served cold.

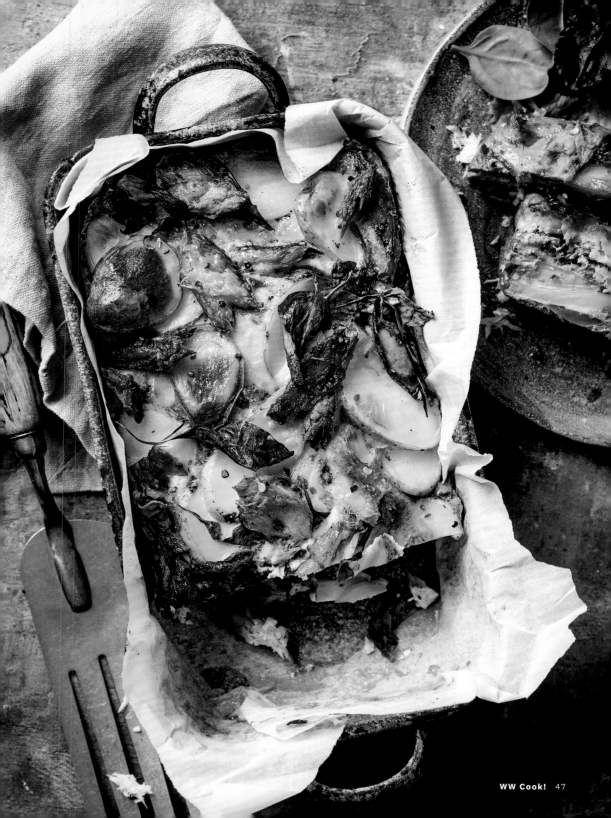

Smoked haddock & potato hash

serves 4   **prep time 15 minutes**   **cook time 45 minutes**

A mildly spiced dish that's great for a weekend brunch or lunch.

600g new potatoes
4 x 120g smoked haddock fillets
2 shallots, finely chopped
3 tomatoes, roughly chopped

FROM THE STORECUPBOARD
Calorie controlled cooking spray
2 garlic cloves, finely chopped
1 tablespoon mild curry powder

TO SERVE (optional)
Chopped fresh flat-leaf parsley

1 Preheat the oven to 200°C, fan 180°C, gas mark 6. Put the potatoes in a pan of cold, salted water. Bring to the boil, then simmer for 30-35 minutes until tender. Drain and set aside for 2 minutes to steam dry in the pan, then roughly chop.

2 Meanwhile, put the haddock fillets on a baking tray, mist with cooking spray and season to taste. Roast for 10 minutes until cooked through. Cool slightly, then flake into pieces and set aside.

3 Put a large nonstick frying pan over a medium-low heat and mist with cooking spray. Fry the shallots and garlic for 8 minutes until starting to soften.

4 Add the potatoes to the pan and sprinkle over the curry powder. Lightly crush the potatoes with a masher and fry for 5 minutes until they start to crisp up. Add the chopped tomatoes to the pan and cook for a further 2 minutes.

5 Fold the fish through the hash and divide between plates. Season to taste and serve.

 SmartPoints value per serving

Cook's tip
If you don't have shallots, a small onion will work just as well in this recipe.

Spicy prawn laksa

serves 4   **prep time 5 minutes**   **cook time 20 minutes**

This spicy, soupy noodle dish is full of Asian-style flavour and couldn't be simpler.

4 tablespoons Thai green curry paste

200ml reduced-fat coconut milk

200g rice noodles

165g peeled raw king prawns

175g baby corn, halved lengthways

FROM THE STORECUPBOARD

400ml fish stock, made with 1 stock cube

1 tablespoon soy sauce

TO SERVE (optional)

Fresh coriander leaves

1 In a large pan, whisk together the curry paste, coconut milk, stock and soy sauce until well combined. Bring to the boil, then gently simmer for 15 minutes.

2 Meanwhile, cook the noodles to pack instructions, then drain and divide between 4 bowls.

3 Add the prawns and baby corn to the coconut broth and poach for 3-5 minutes until the prawns have turned pink. Divide between the bowls, pouring it over the noodles, then serve.

9 SmartPoints value per serving

Cook's tip
Remember that prawns should be pink all over to ensure they are properly cooked through.

Cod with braised bacon lentils

serves 4   prep time 15 minutes   cook time 45 minutes

Punchy flavours of bacon and pesto make this dish something special.

100g lean smoked bacon medallions, finely chopped

1 red onion, finely chopped

2 carrots, finely chopped

2 x 400g tins green lentils, drained and rinsed

4 x 140g skinless cod loin fillets

FROM THE STORECUPBOARD

Calorie controlled cooking spray

400ml hot vegetable stock, made with 1 stock cube

1 teaspoon dried mixed herbs

1 tablespoon red wine vinegar

TO SERVE (optional)

Chopped fresh flat-leaf parsley

1   Mist a medium nonstick pan or flameproof casserole with cooking spray and fry the bacon over a medium heat for 5 minutes, until golden. Add the onion and carrots and cook, covered, for 10 minutes until starting to soften – you'll need to add a splash of water to the pan to prevent sticking.

2   Add the lentils, stock, dried mixed herbs and red wine vinegar to the pan. Bring to the boil, then reduce the heat and simmer, uncovered, for 20 minutes, until most of the liquid has evaporated and the lentils are tender.

3   Add 150ml boiling water to the pan, stir to combine, then arrange the cod on top of the lentils. Season, then cover and cook over a low heat for 8 minutes until the fish is cooked through, then serve.

 SmartPoints value per serving

Cook's tip
If you want to use dried lentils in this recipe, you'll need 200g, cooked to pack instructions.

Tuna, green bean & bulgur wheat salad

serves 4　　**prep time 10 minutes**　　**cook time 20 minutes**

This Middle-Eastern inspired salad makes a great-tasting lunch.

150g bulgur wheat
300g green beans, trimmed
2 tablespoons tahini
Grated zest and juice of 1 lemon
2 x 160g tins tuna in spring water, drained and flaked

FROM THE STORECUPBOARD
1 teaspoon clear honey

TO SERVE (optional)
Chopped fresh flat-leaf parsley

1　Cook the bulgur wheat to pack instructions, then set aside to cool.

2　Bring a pan of water to the boil and cook the beans for 2 minutes. Drain and rinse under cold running water to stop them from cooking further. Put the beans in a large bowl with the bulgur wheat and toss together.

3　In a separate bowl, whisk together the tahini, lemon zest and juice, honey and 2 tablespoons water, then season to taste.

4　Fold the tuna through the beans and bulgur wheat and divide between serving plates. Drizzle with the dressing and serve.

 5　**SmartPoints value per serving**

Cook's tip
Make this recipe gluten free by swapping the bulgur wheat for the same quantity of quinoa, cooked to pack instructions, for no extra SmartPoints per serving.

Spiced salmon & rice salad

serves 4   prep time 20 minutes + cooling & standing   cook time 25 minutes

This easy, rice-based salmon salad packs in plenty of spicy flavour.

300g mixed basmati and wild rice

4 x 120g skinless salmon fillets

1 cucumber, halved lengthways, deseeded and cut into chunks

Grated zest and juice of 1 lemon, plus lemon wedges, to serve

4 tablespoons 0% fat natural Greek yogurt

FROM THE STORECUPBOARD

½ teaspoon paprika

½ teaspoon cayenne pepper

½ teaspoon ground cumin

Calorie controlled cooking spray

1   Preheat the oven to 180°C, fan 160°C, gas mark 4. Cook the rice to pack instructions, then drain and leave to cool.

2   In a small bowl, mix together the paprika, cayenne pepper and cumin. Put the salmon fillets on a baking tray, mist with cooking spray, then sprinkle with the spice mix. Roast for 8-10 minutes until the fish is cooked through and starts to flake.

3   Leave to cool, then transfer to the fridge to chill for 10 minutes before flaking into chunks. In a large bowl, mix the cucumber with half the lemon juice and season to taste. Leave to stand for 10 minutes, then drain.

4   In a separate bowl, whisk together the remaining lemon juice, the zest and yogurt.

5   Add the rice and salmon chunks to the cucumber and mix gently. Spoon onto a large platter and serve drizzled with the yogurt dressing.

   8   SmartPoints value per serving

Cook's tip

You could replace the rice with a 400g tin of drained and rinsed green lentils, for a total of 0 SmartPoints per serving.

Crispy sea bass with sesame noodles

serves 4   prep time 25 minutes   cook time 15 minutes

Asian-style noodles are the perfect partner for the sea bass in this easy recipe.

200g wholewheat noodles
4 x 90g sea bass fillets
**5cm piece fresh ginger,
finely chopped**
1 tablespoon sesame seeds
4 pak choi, leaves separated

FROM THE STORECUPBOARD
½ tablespoon vegetable oil
Calorie-controlled cooking spray
1 garlic clove, finely chopped
1 teaspoon dried chilli flakes
1 tablespoon soy sauce

1 Cook the noodles to pack instructions, then drain and set aside.

2 Pat the sea bass fillets dry with kitchen paper. Heat the oil in a large, non-stick frying pan over a medium-high heat and cook the fish, skin-side down, for 2 minutes, pressing it down with a spatula until the skin is crisp. Gently flip the fish and cook for a further 2 minutes until it starts to flake. Transfer to a warm plate and leave to rest for 5 minutes.

3 Meanwhile, mist the frying pan with cooking spray, add the ginger and garlic and fry for 2 minutes. Add the sesame seeds, chilli flakes and pak choi to the pan, and cook for 2 minutes. Add the noodles and cook, stirring, until the noodles are heated through, then stir in the soy sauce. Serve the noodles topped with the sea bass.

 SmartPoints value per serving

Cook's tip
Cooking the fish with the skin on adds flavour and helps stop the delicate fillets from falling apart. Don't move the fish around once it's in the pan – you only need to turn it once.

Salmon & dill pasta

serves 4   prep time 10 minutes   cook time 15 minutes

For a quick and easy lunch, this tasty pasta dish is hard to beat.

240g fusilli

**4 tablespoons half-fat
crème fraîche**

Grated zest and juice of ½ lemon

**4 x 120g cooked skinless salmon
fillets, flaked**

**15g fresh dill, fronds picked
and finely chopped, plus extra
to garnish**

FROM THE STORECUPBOARD
1 teaspoon Dijon mustard

TO SERVE (optional)
Steamed Tenderstem broccoli

1   Cook the pasta to pack instructions. Drain, reserving 50ml of
the cooking water, and return to the pan.

2   In a bowl, whisk together the crème fraîche, lemon zest and
juice and the mustard. Mix into the pasta with the reserved
pasta water to help create a smooth sauce. Gently stir in the
salmon and dill, season to taste, then divide between bowls,
scatter over the extra dill and serve.

8   **SmartPoints value per serving**

Cook's tip
Boost your fibre intake by
swapping the regular fusilli
for a wholewheat version,
or any other wholewheat
pasta. The SmartPoints
will remain the same.

Veggie

Broccoli & Cheddar quiche

serves 6 **prep time 15 minutes** **cook time 50 minutes** **freezable**

Classic flavours combine in this easy quiche, perfect for a light lunch.

375g sheet shortcrust pastry (225g used)

350g broccoli, broken into florets and stems roughly chopped

3 eggs

75g half-fat crème fraîche

50g half-fat Cheddar, grated

FROM THE STORECUPBOARD
2 teaspoons Dijon mustard

TO SERVE (optional)
Mixed salad leaves

1 Preheat the oven to 200°C, fan 180°C, gas mark 6. Unroll the pastry sheet, then use a rolling pin to roll it out further so that it's large enough to line a 21cm shallow, loose-bottom tart tin. Trim and discard the excess pastry, then line the pastry case with baking paper. Fill with baking beans or rice and blind bake for 15 minutes. Remove the beans and baking paper, then bake for a further 5-8 minutes, until golden.

2 Meanwhile, blanch the broccoli in a pan of boiling water for 3-5 minutes, until just tender. Drain and refresh under cold running water, then pat dry with kitchen paper and set aside.

3 In a jug, whisk together the eggs, crème fraîche, mustard and 40g of the cheese.

4 Scatter the broccoli over the base of the blind-baked pastry case then pour over the egg mixture. Scatter over the remaining cheese and bake for 25 minutes until the filling is set but still wobbles slightly in the centre when gently shaken.

5 Remove from the oven and let cool slightly before releasing from the tin and serving.

The quiche can be frozen in an airtight container for up to 3 months.

8   **SmartPoints value per serving**

Cook's tip
Top the quiche with 100g halved cherry tomatoes before baking, for no extra SmartPoints.

Baked potatoes with ricotta & roasted tomatoes

serves 4   prep time 10 minutes   **cook time** 1 hour 20 minutes

Expand your potato topping repertoire with this simple yet classic combination.

4 x 180g baking potatoes
320g cherry tomatoes
2 sprigs fresh thyme
75g ricotta

FROM THE STORECUPBOARD
Calorie controlled cooking spray
1½ teaspoons olive oil
1½ teaspoons balsamic vinegar

TO SERVE (optional)
Mixed salad leaves

1   Preheat the oven to 200°C, fan 180°C, gas mark 6. Prick the potatoes all over with a fork, put on a baking tray and mist with cooking spray. Bake for 1 hour 20 minutes, until tender with a crisp, golden skin.

2   Meanwhile, put the tomatoes and thyme in a small baking dish and drizzle over the oil and balsamic vinegar. Season to taste and toss to coat. Bake alongside the potatoes for the final 35 minutes of cooking time.

3   Remove the potatoes and tomatoes from the oven, and discard the thyme. Split the potatoes and top with the ricotta and roasted tomatoes. Drizzle over any juices from the baking dish, season with freshly ground black pepper and serve.

9   **SmartPoints value per serving**

Cook's tip
The fresh thyme really boosts the flavour of the roasted tomatoes. You could also use fresh rosemary.

Spicy lentil & chickpea soup

serves 4   **prep time 5 minutes**   **cook time 30 minutes**   **freezable**

Red lentils and chickpeas make this soup really hearty and satisfying.

1 onion, roughly chopped

**250g dried red lentils, rinsed
under cold running water**

**400g tin chickpeas, drained
and rinsed**

1½ tablespoons harissa paste

**4 tablespoons 0% fat natural
Greek yogurt**

FROM THE STORECUPBOARD

½ tablespoon olive oil

1 teaspoon ground cumin

**1.5 litres vegetable stock, made
with 2 stock cubes**

1   Heat the oil in a medium pan set over a medium heat. Cook the onion, stirring, for 6-8 minutes until just starting to soften. Stir in the cumin and cook for 1 minute.

2   Add the lentils and stir to combine, then pour in the stock. Bring the mixture to the boil, then reduce the heat and simmer for 15 minutes or until the lentils are tender.

3   Remove from the heat and use a stick blender to blitz to a thick soup.

4   Return the pan to the heat, stir in the chickpeas and 1 tablespoon of the harissa paste, then simmer for 5 minutes until hot. Season to taste.

5   Ladle into bowls and serve topped with the yogurt and the remaining harissa paste.

The soup can be frozen in an airtight container for up to 3 months.

 SmartPoints value per serving

Cook's tip

Give the soup a flavour boost by adding some chopped fresh coriander just before serving.

Lentil, feta & tomato salad

serves 4   prep time 5 minutes

Put this tasty salad together in next to no time – there's no cooking required!

2 x 400g tins green lentils, drained and rinsed

400g baby plum tomatoes, halved

25g fresh flat-leaf parsley, leaves picked and roughly chopped

160g light feta

3 x 20g sachets WW Garlic & Chive Dressing

1   Put the lentils, tomatoes and parsley in a medium bowl. Crumble over the feta, then drizzle over the dressing and toss to combine. Season to taste.

2   Divide the salad between bowls and serve seasoned with freshly ground black pepper.

3   **SmartPoints value per serving**

Cook's tip
You could bulk up this meal by adding 1 sliced cooked skinless chicken breast per serving, for no extra SmartPoints.

Courgette & lentil lasagne

serves 4   **prep time 20 minutes**   **cook time 55 minutes**   **freezable**

Perfect for a meat-free family dinner, this veggie lasagne is full of flavour.

3 courgettes, trimmed and thinly sliced
2 x 400g tins green lentils, drained and rinsed
500g passata
200g wholewheat lasagne sheets
375g light mozzarella, roughly torn

FROM THE STORECUPBOARD
Calorie controlled cooking spray
2 garlic cloves, finely chopped
1 tablespoon balsamic vinegar
1 teaspoon dried mixed herbs

TO SERVE (optional)
Mixed salad leaves

1   Mist a large nonstick frying pan with cooking spray and cook the courgettes over a high heat for 10 minutes, stirring occasionally, until softened. Remove from the heat, stir in the lentils and set aside.

2   Mist a medium nonstick pan with cooking spray and set over a medium heat. Fry the garlic for 1 minute, then add the passata and heat until just beginning to simmer. Stir in the balsamic vinegar and dried herbs, then season to taste and remove from the heat. Preheat the oven to 200°C, fan 180°C, gas mark 6.

3   Assemble the lasagne. Spoon a little of the passata into a 1.5-litre baking dish and spread over the base of the dish, then layer with one-quarter of the lasagne sheets, followed by one-quarter of the passata sauce. Scatter over one-third of the courgette and lentil mixture, followed by one-quarter of the mozzarella. Repeat twice, then add a final layer of lasagne sheets, passata and mozzarella.

4   Cover with kitchen foil and bake for 30 minutes, then remove the foil and bake for a further 15 minutes, until the pasta is cooked through and the cheese is melted and bubbling, then serve.

The lasagne can be frozen in an airtight container for up to 3 months.

 SmartPoints value per serving

Cook's tip
Make sure to start the lasagne with a thin layer of passata sauce – it will stop the pasta from sticking to the baking dish.

Oven-baked red pepper risotto

serves 4   prep time 5 minutes   cook time 35 minutes

This delicious, fuss-free baked risotto takes just a few minutes to prepare.

1 onion, finely chopped
275g risotto rice
150g roasted red peppers in brine, drained and cut into thin strips
400g tin chopped tomatoes
75g light mozzarella, torn

FROM THE STORECUPBOARD
Calorie controlled cooking spray
1 garlic clove, finely chopped
450ml hot vegetable stock, made with 1 stock cube

TO SERVE (optional)
Chopped fresh flat-leaf parsley
Mixed salad leaves

1 Preheat the oven to 200°C, fan 180°C, gas mark 6. Mist a medium nonstick ovenproof frying pan or flameproof casserole with cooking spray and cook the onion over a medium heat for 6-8 minutes, stirring occasionally, until starting to soften. Add the garlic and cook for a further 1 minute.

2 Add the rice and cook, stirring, for 1 minute, then stir in the red peppers, tomatoes and 375ml of the vegetable stock. Bring to the boil, then cover and transfer to the oven. Bake for 20-25 minutes, until the rice is tender and the liquid is completely absorbed.

3 Remove from the oven, add the remaining stock and three-quarters of the mozzarella and stir until the cheese is melted. Season and top with the remaining mozzarella. Serve seasoned with freshly ground black pepper.

  SmartPoints value per serving

Cook's tip
You could spice this dish up by adding 1 teaspoon of chilli flakes when you add the garlic to the pan, for no extra SmartPoints.

Spiced sweet potato salad

serves 4   prep time 10 minutes   cook time 25 minutes

A vibrant, flavoursome salad that's lightly spiced with paprika and za'atar.

500g sweet potatoes, peeled, and cut into 2cm chunks

1 medium avocado, peeled, stone removed and diced (150g prepared weight)

150g mixed salad leaves

40g light feta

FROM THE STORECUPBOARD
Calorie controlled cooking spray
1½ teaspoons za'atar
½ teaspoon paprika
2 teaspoons olive oil
1½ teaspoons cider vinegar

1 Preheat the oven to 200°C, fan 180°C, gas mark 6. Put the sweet potatoes on a large baking tray, mist with cooking spray, scatter over the spices and season to taste. Toss to coat, then roast for 25 minutes, turning halfway, until crisp and golden.

2 In a small bowl, whisk together the oil and cider vinegar, then season to taste. Put the avocado and salad leaves in a medium bowl, then drizzle over the dressing and toss to coat.

3 Transfer the salad to a large serving platter, top with the spiced sweet potato, then crumble over the feta and serve.

 SmartPoints value per serving

Cook's tip
This salad is best served while the sweet potato is still warm.

Cauliflower 'rice' burrito bowls

serves 4   prep time 10 minutes   cook time 5 minutes

Want something quick? These colourful veggie bowls are ready in only 15 minutes.

600g cauliflower

2 x 400g tins black beans, drained and rinsed

340g tin sweetcorn, drained

1 medium avocado, peeled, stone removed and thinly sliced (150g prepared weight)

4 tablespoons tomato salsa

FROM THE STORECUPBOARD
Calorie controlled cooking spray
¾ teaspoon ground coriander
¾ teaspoon ground cumin
¾ teaspoon paprika
1½ tablespoons olive oil
2 teaspoons red wine vinegar

TO SERVE (optional)
Fresh coriander leaves

1   Use a food processor to whizz the cauliflower to a rice-like texture. If you don't have a food processor, you can grate the cauliflower using the coarse side of a cheese grater.

2   Mist a large nonstick frying pan with cooking spray and cook the cauliflower 'rice', stirring, over a medium heat for 5 minutes until tender. Transfer the cauliflower to a large bowl, add the spices and ½ tablespoon of the olive oil, then season to taste and stir to combine.

3   Divide the spiced cauliflower between 4 bowls and top with the black beans, sweetcorn and avocado.

4   In a small bowl, whisk the remaining oil with the vinegar, then season to taste. Drizzle the dressing over the burrito bowls and serve topped with the salsa.

5   SmartPoints value per serving

Cook's tip

Don't over-process the cauliflower – it should be the texture of rice or couscous. Using a cheese grater will give you a slightly chunkier texture. To save time, you could use 2 x 300g packs prepared cauliflower rice.

Mushroom, cashew & black bean stir-fry

serves 4   prep time 5 minutes   cook time 25 minutes

Toasted cashews add flavour and crunch to this simple veggie stir-fry.

200g dried rice noodles
60g unsalted cashew nuts
500g chestnut mushrooms, thickly sliced
320g pack prepared stir-fry vegetables
4 tablespoons black bean stir-fry sauce

FROM THE STORECUPBOARD
Calorie controlled cooking spray
1 teaspoon chilli flakes

TO SERVE (optional)
Fresh coriander sprigs

1 Prepare the rice noodles to pack instructions, then drain and set aside.

2 Heat a large nonstick wok or frying pan over a high heat and toast the cashew nuts for 1-2 minutes. Remove from the wok and set aside to cool slightly before roughly chopping.

3 Mist the wok with cooking spray and stir-fry the mushrooms and chilli flakes for 10 minutes until the mushrooms are tender and golden – you may need to add a splash of water to stop the mushrooms from sticking.

4 Add the prepared vegetables to the wok and stir-fry for 5 minutes, then add the noodles, toasted cashews and black bean sauce. Stir-fry for 1-2 minutes until well combined, then serve.

9   SmartPoints value per serving

Cook's tip
You could use any mushrooms you like in this stir-fry – try oyster mushrooms for a more delicate flavour, or shiitake mushrooms for a richer, buttery flavour.

Pea, leek & goat's cheese baked omelette

serves 4   prep time 10 minutes   cook time 40 minutes

This easy omelette is served with paprika-spiced sweet potato wedges.

380g sweet potatoes, scrubbed and cut into thin wedges
2 leeks, trimmed and thinly sliced
150g frozen peas
8 eggs
75g goat's cheese

FROM THE STORECUPBOARD
Calorie controlled cooking spray
½ teaspoon paprika
Freshly ground black pepper

TO SERVE (optional)
Mixed salad leaves

1   Preheat the oven to 200°C, fan 180°C, gas mark 6. Put the sweet potatoes on a large baking tray and mist with cooking spray. Scatter over the paprika, season to taste and bake for 40 minutes, turning halfway, until crisp and golden.

2   Meanwhile, mist a medium, nonstick ovenproof frying pan with cooking spray and put over a medium heat. Fry the leeks for 8-10 minutes until softened. Add the peas to the pan and cook for 1 minute, then remove from the heat and set aside.

3   Crack the eggs into a large jug, season to taste and whisk until just frothy. Pour over the leeks and gently stir to combine. Crumble over the goat's cheese and transfer to the oven. Cook alongside the wedges for 15-20 minutes, until the egg is set.

4   Cut the omelette into wedges and season with freshly ground black pepper. Serve with the sweet potato wedges on the side.

5   SmartPoints value per serving

Cook's tip
If you don't like the flavour of goat's cheese, you could use the same quantity of light feta instead for a total of 4 SmartPoints per serving.

Butternut squash & tofu Thai curry

serves 4 **prep time 10 minutes** **cook time 35 minutes** **freezable**

A ready-made curry paste makes this vegan dish super-simple to prepare.

800g butternut squash, peeled, deseeded and cut into 2cm chunks

280g firm tofu, cut into 2cm chunks

3 tablespoons vegan Thai green curry paste

½ x 400g tin reduced-fat coconut milk

240g brown basmati rice

FROM THE STORECUPBOARD
Calorie controlled cooking spray
200ml vegetable stock, made with ½ stock cube

TO SERVE (optional)
Finely chopped fresh coriander

1 Mist a large nonstick lidded wok or frying pan with cooking spray and put over a medium heat, then stir-fry the butternut squash for 5 minutes, until starting to soften.

2 Add the tofu and curry paste, and stir-fry for 3 minutes, then pour in the stock and coconut milk. Stir to combine and bring to a simmer. Cover and cook for 20-25 minutes until the squash is tender.

3 Meanwhile, cook the rice to pack instructions.

4 Remove the lid from the curry and, using a wooden spoon, press 6 of the squash pieces against the side of the wok. Stir the mashed squash into the curry to thicken the sauce, then season to taste.

5 Serve the rice with the curry.

The curry can be frozen in an airtight container for up to 3 months.

9 SmartPoints value per serving

Cook's tip
If you prefer a less spicy dish, use the same quantity of red curry paste instead of green, for no extra SmartPoints.

Sticky glazed aubergines

serves 4   prep time 15 minutes   cook time 1 hour

Glazed aubergines take centre stage in this delicious Asian-inspired dish.

4 small aubergines

240g basmati rice

4 spring onions, trimmed and thinly sliced

1 red chilli, thinly sliced

½ teaspoon toasted sesame seeds

FROM THE STORECUPBOARD

Calorie controlled cooking spray

3 tablespoons clear honey

3 tablespoons soy sauce

½ teaspoon chilli flakes

TO SERVE (optional)

Chopped fresh coriander

1   Preheat the oven to 200°C, fan 180°C, gas mark 6, and line a large baking tray with baking paper. Halve the aubergines lengthways and score the flesh in a criss-cross pattern. Put on the prepared baking tray, mist with cooking spray and bake for 45 minutes, until tender.

2   Make the glaze: combine the honey, soy sauce and chilli flakes in a small bowl. Brush one-third of the mixture over the aubergine halves and bake for another 5 minutes. Repeat twice, until all the glaze is used and the aubergines are tender and sticky.

3   Meanwhile, cook the rice to pack instructions.

4   Serve the rice and glazed aubergines garnished with the spring onions, chilli and sesame seeds.

 SmartPoints value per serving

Cook's tip

If you can't find ready-toasted sesame seeds, put untoasted ones in a dry frying pan and toast over a medium heat, stirring, for 3-5 minutes until golden.

Mixed bean chilli

serves 4   **prep time** 5 minutes   **cook time** 25 minutes   **freezable**

This colourful chilli is quick and easy to make, and is perfect for batch cooking.

3 mixed peppers, deseeded and thinly sliced

400g tin chopped tomatoes

2 x 400g tins mixed beans, drained and rinsed

2 x 250g pouches microwave brown basmati rice

FROM THE STORECUPBOARD

Calorie controlled cooking spray

2 teaspoons paprika

1 teaspoon mild chilli powder

1 teaspoon ground cumin

100ml vegetable stock, made with ½ stock cube

TO SERVE (optional)

Fresh coriander

1   Mist a large nonstick frying pan with cooking spray and fry the peppers over a high heat for 5-7 minutes, until starting to soften. Stir in the paprika, chilli powder and cumin, then season to taste and cook for a further 1 minute.

2   Add the tomatoes and stock, then bring the mixture to a simmer. Cook for 10-12 minutes, until the mixture has thickened slightly. Stir in the mixed beans and simmer for a further 5 minutes.

3   Cook the rice to pack instructions and divide it between 4 bowls, then top with the chilli and serve.

The chilli can be frozen in an airtight container for up to 3 months.

   SmartPoints value per serving

Cook's tip

If you prefer a thicker sauce, use a stick blender to purée a cupful of the chilli in a small bowl, then stir the purée back into the pan.

Meat

Steak & potato salad

serves 4   prep time 10 minutes + resting   cook time 45 minutes

This warm salad is a deliciously different way to serve steak and potatoes.

350g potatoes, peeled
and cut into 1cm cubes

4 x 125g lean minute
thin-cut steaks

4 x 20g sachets WW Classic
Garlic & Chive Dressing

250g cherry tomatoes, halved

200g mixed salad leaves

FROM THE STORECUPBOARD
Calorie controlled cooking spray

2 teaspoons Dijon mustard

1 Preheat the oven to 200°C, fan 180°C, gas mark 6. Put the potatoes on a large baking tray, mist with cooking spray and season to taste. Bake for 40 minutes, turning halfway, until crisp and golden.

2 Meanwhile, heat a large nonstick frying pan over a high heat. Mist the steaks with cooking spray and season to taste. In batches, sear the steaks for 1 minute on each side, then remove from the pan and rest for 5 minutes before cutting into thick strips.

3 In a small bowl, whisk together the WW Classic Garlic & Chive Dressing, mustard and 2 teaspoons of cold water. Set aside.

4 Divide the tomatoes and salad leaves between plates, top with the steak and potato cubes and serve with the salad dressing drizzled over.

 SmartPoints value per serving

Cook's tip
Make this extra special by crumbling over 20g Stilton per serving for an extra 4 SmartPoints per serving.

Teriyaki beef stir-fry

serves 4   prep time 5 minutes   cook time 10 minutes

Classic Japanese-style flavours in a simple stir-fry that's ready in just 15 minutes.

**500g lean sirloin steak,
thinly sliced**

200g dried egg noodles

3cm piece fresh ginger, grated

**300g green beans, trimmed and
cut into 2cm pieces**

3 tablespoons teriyaki sauce

FROM THE STORECUPBOARD

½ teaspoon chilli flakes

1 tablespoon sunflower oil

1   Put the steak in a medium bowl, add the chilli flakes, then season and toss to combine. Set aside until needed.

2   Cook the egg noodles to pack instructions, then drain and set aside.

3   Meanwhile, heat the oil in a large nonstick wok or frying pan and stir-fry the ginger over a high heat for 30 seconds. Add the beans and stir-fry for 3-5 minutes, then remove from the wok and set aside.

4   Increase the heat to high, then stir-fry the beef in batches, for 1-2 minutes.

5   Return the beans to the wok along with the noodles and teriyaki sauce, and toss to combine. Stir-fry for 1-2 minutes until hot, then remove from the heat and serve.

  SmartPoints value per serving

Cook's tip

Stir-fries are great for using up any extra veg that you have in the fridge, such as peppers, mushrooms and broccoli.

Sloppy joes with butternut squash wedges

serves 4   prep time 15 minutes   cook time 45 minutes   freezable

Fancy a change from burgers? Try this classic North American recipe.

1 butternut squash (900g), unpeeled, deseeded and cut into wedges

500g 5% fat beef mince

400g tin chopped tomatoes

4 x 60g hamburger buns, cut in half

1 Little Gem lettuce, leaves separated

FROM THE STORECUPBOARD

1 tablespoon olive oil

½ teaspoon chilli flakes

1 teaspoon dried mixed herbs

Calorie controlled cooking spray

1 garlic clove, finely chopped

200ml beef stock, made with 1 stock cube

1   Preheat the oven to 200°C, fan 180°C, gas mark 6. Spread the butternut squash wedges out on a baking tray. Drizzle with the olive oil and scatter over the chilli flakes and half the dried mixed herbs. Toss to coat and season to taste. Roast for 40-45 minutes until golden and softened.

2   Meanwhile, put a nonstick frying pan over a high heat and mist with cooking spray. Add the mince, breaking up with a wooden spoon, and fry until golden brown. Drain off any excess fat.

3   Add the garlic and cook for 1 minute, then add the chopped tomatoes, the remaining dried mixed herbs and the beef stock. Bring to the boil, then simmer for 20 minutes until reduced.

4   Lightly toast the cut sides of the buns and top with the lettuce and mince. Serve with the butternut squash wedges.

 SmartPoints value per serving

Cook's tip
Add a tin of drained and rinsed kidney beans to the mince mixture for a chilli con carne twist. The SmartPoints will remain the same.

Lamb & green bean stew

serves 4   prep time 15 minutes   cook time 1 hour 25 minutes   freezable

This hearty stew makes a satisfying meal for colder evenings.

450g lean lamb leg steak, cut into 2cm chunks
600g baby potatoes, halved
400g tin chopped tomatoes
320g green beans, trimmed and cut into 3cm pieces

FROM THE STORECUPBOARD
Calorie controlled cooking spray
300ml lamb stock, made with 1 stock cube
2 teaspoons dried mixed herbs
2 bay leaves
Freshly ground black pepper

TO SERVE (optional)
200g sourdough bread

1   Mist a large flameproof casserole with cooking spray and set over a medium-high heat. Season the lamb and sear for 3-5 minutes until browned all over – you may need to do this in batches.

2   Add the potatoes, tomatoes, stock, dried mixed herbs and bay leaves to the casserole, then season to taste and stir to combine. Bring to the boil, then reduce the heat, cover and simmer for 1 hour.

3   Add the beans to the casserole and continue to cook, covered, for 15 minutes until the beans are tender.

4   Serve the stew with a sprinkling of freshly ground black pepper.

The stew can be frozen in an airtight container for up to 3 months.

  SmartPoints value per serving

Cook's tip
Bulk this out with a tin of drained and rinsed butter beans. Add them with the green beans for no extra SmartPoints.

Easy carbonara

serves 4   **prep time 15 minutes**   **cook time 20 minutes**

This simple pasta dish is an all-time Italian classic.

1 onion, finely chopped
100g bacon medallions, cut into 1cm chunks
240g spaghetti
3 egg yolks, beaten
40g Parmesan, finely grated

FROM THE STORECUPBOARD
Calorie controlled cooking spray
2 garlic cloves, unpeeled
Freshly ground black pepper

TO SERVE (optional)
Rocket

1 Mist a nonstick frying pan with cooking spray and set over a medium heat. Add the onion, and cook for 6-8 minutes until softened, adding a splash of water if it starts to stick. Gently crush the garlic cloves with the back of a spoon, then add them to the pan along with the bacon. Cook for a further 5 minutes until the bacon is golden. Remove and discard the garlic cloves.

2 Meanwhile, cook the spaghetti to pack instructions. Drain, reserving 100ml of the cooking water, and return to the pan.

3 Add the bacon and onion mixture, the egg yolks and Parmesan to the pasta and stir to combine, allowing the heat from the pasta to cook the egg and form a sauce. Add a little of the reserved pasta water to thin the sauce so it coats the spaghetti. Season to taste, then serve sprinkled with more freshly ground black pepper.

 8   **SmartPoints value per serving**

Cook's tip
Try adding some sliced button mushrooms to the pan with the onion for no extra SmartPoints.

Smoky BBQ sausages with butternut squash mash

serves 4   **prep time** **15 minutes**   **cook time** **35 minutes**

Try this delicious twist on traditional bangers and mash.

8 reduced-fat pork sausages

4 x 15g sachets WW Smoky BBQ Sauce

1kg butternut squash, peeled, deseeded and cut into 3cm chunks

1 tablespoon low-fat spread

300g young leaf spinach

FROM THE STORECUPBOARD
Calorie controlled cooking spray
½ teaspoon chilli flakes

1   Preheat the oven to 200°C, fan 180°C, gas mark 6. Put the sausages into a roasting tin, mist with cooking spray and bake for 25 minutes. Brush the sausages with the WW Smoky BBQ Sauce and continue to bake for 7-10 minutes, until cooked through.

2   Meanwhile, put the butternut squash in a large pan, cover with cold water and bring to the boil. Cook for 15-20 minutes, until tender, then drain and mash with the low-fat spread. Season to taste and keep warm while you prepare the spinach.

3   Wilt the spinach with a splash of water in a large pan set over a medium heat – you may need to do this in batches. Drain any excess liquid from the pan, then add the chilli flakes. Season to taste and stir to combine.

4   Serve the sausages and mash with the spinach on the side.

 SmartPoints value per serving

Cook's tip
When boiling the butternut squash, try adding 4-5 whole garlic cloves, then mash together with the squash.

Zesty pork with spinach & butter beans

serves 4   prep time 10 minutes + marinating & resting   cook time 30 minutes

Tender pork fillet is marinated then roasted for maximum flavour in this tasty dish.

550g pork tenderloin fillet, fat trimmed

100g pouch WW Zesty Lemon & Herb Marinade

400g young leaf spinach

2 x 400g tins butter beans, drained and rinsed

Grated zest and juice of ½ lemon, plus lemon wedges, to serve

FROM THE STORECUPBOARD
Calorie controlled cooking spray

1   Put the pork in a shallow bowl and pour over the WW Zesty Lemon & Herb Marinade. Turn to coat, then cover and set aside to marinate at room temperature for 20 minutes.

2   Preheat the oven to 220°C, fan 200°C, gas mark 7. Heat a large nonstick frying pan over a high heat, then mist with cooking spray. Sear the pork fillet for 5 minutes, turning frequently, until browned all over. Remove the pork from the pan and wrap in kitchen foil. Put on a baking tray and roast for 18-20 minutes, turning halfway. Remove from the oven and set aside to rest for 5 minutes, then remove the foil and cut into 12 equal slices.

3   While the pork is resting, wilt the spinach with a splash of water in a large pan set over a medium heat – you may need to do this in batches. Drain any excess liquid from the pan, then add the butter beans and season to taste. Stir to combine, then remove from the heat and stir in the lemon zest and juice.

4   Divide the spinach and butter beans between 4 plates, top with the pork and serve.

Cook's tip
You could also serve this with some crusty bread – a 50g slice will add 4 SmartPoints per serving.

3   **SmartPoints value per serving**

Thai beef salad

serves 4   prep time 10 minutes + resting   cook time 10 minutes

An irresistible beef and noodle dish that's ready in a flash.

200g dried rice noodles

Grated zest and juice of ½ lime, plus extra lime wedges, to serve

450g lean rump steak

6 spring onions, trimmed and finely sliced

1 red chilli, deseeded and finely chopped

FROM THE STORECUPBOARD

1 tablespoon vegetable oil

2 tablespoons soy sauce

½ tablespoon clear honey

Calorie controlled cooking spray

1   Cook the rice noodles to pack instructions, then drain and set aside in a medium bowl.

2   To make the dressing, put the lime zest and juice, vegetable oil, soy sauce and honey in a small bowl, and stir to combine. Pour three-quarters of the dressing over the noodles and toss to coat.

3   Heat a large nonstick frying pan over a high heat. Mist the steaks with cooking spray and season to taste. In batches, sear the steaks for 1-2 minutes on each side, or until cooked to your liking, then remove from the pan and let rest for 5 minutes before cutting into thick strips.

4   Divide the noodles between bowls, top with the steak and garnish with the spring onions and chilli. Drizzle over the remaining dressing and serve with the lime wedges on the side.

  SmartPoints value per serving

Cook's tip
You could replace the beef with the same quantity of skinless chicken breast fillets, for 7 SmartPoints per serving.

Korean crispy beef

serves 4   **prep time** 10 minutes   **cook time** 20 minutes

This recipe is inspired by bibimbap, the popular meat and rice dish from Korea.

200g jasmine rice

500g extra-lean 5% fat beef mince

1 cucumber, halved and deseeded

1 tablespoon sesame seeds

4 eggs

FROM THE STORECUPBOARD

Calorie controlled cooking spray

2 garlic cloves, finely chopped

1 tablespoon vegetable oil

1 tablespoon cider vinegar

1 tablespoon soy sauce

1   Cook the rice to pack instructions, then fluff the grains up using a fork.

2   Meanwhile, mist a large nonstick wok or frying pan with cooking spray and stir-fry the mince and garlic over a medium-high heat for 10 minutes, until the beef is crisp.

3   While the rice and beef are cooking, use a rolling pin to gently bash the cucumber until it starts to break up, then roughly chop into chunks.

4   Transfer the beef to a dish and keep warm. Put the vegetable oil, vinegar and soy sauce in the wok, then add the cucumber and stir-fry for 5 minutes. Stir in the sesame seeds and remove the wok from the heat.

5   Mist a nonstick frying pan with cooking spray and fry the eggs for 1-2 minutes, until the whites are set and the yolks are soft.

6   Divide the rice between bowls, top with the beef stir-fry, a fried egg and the cucumber, then sprinkle over some freshly ground black pepper to serve.

   SmartPoints value per serving

Cook's tip

Spice up this dish by adding a teaspoon of chilli flakes when cooking the cucumber.

Griddled pork steaks with mint & watermelon salad

serves 4   **prep time** **20 minutes + marinating & resting**   **cook time 15 minutes**

Marinating the pork steaks keeps the meat juicy and tender in this simple dish.

4 lean pork steaks, excess fat trimmed

150g couscous

Juice of ½ lemon

1 small watermelon, peeled and flesh cut into 3cm cubes

35g watercress leaves, roughly chopped

FROM THE STORECUPBOARD

1 tablespoon balsamic vinegar

1 teaspoon clear honey

2 teaspoons cumin seeds

1 vegetable stock cube, crumbled

Calorie controlled cooking spray

TO SERVE (optional)

Fresh mint leaves, roughly chopped

1   In a large non-metallic bowl, mix together the balsamic vinegar and honey, and season to taste. Add the pork steaks and turn to coat. Cover and marinate in the fridge for at least 2 hours or ideally overnight.

2   In a separate bowl, mix together the couscous, cumin seeds and stock cube, then cook to couscous pack instructions. Set aside to cool, then stir through the lemon juice and season to taste.

3   In a serving bowl, mix together the watermelon and watercress and season to taste. Set aside.

4   Set a griddle pan over a high heat and mist with cooking spray. Cook the pork steaks for 5 minutes on each side until cooked through. Transfer to a plate, cover with foil and leave to rest for 5 minutes.

5   Divide the couscous and the watermelon salad between plates, then top with the pork steaks. Drizzle with any juices from the resting plate and serve.

   SmartPoints value per serving

Cook's tip

Bulk up the couscous by adding a tin of drained and rinsed chickpeas. The SmartPoints will remain the same.

Recipe index

SmartPoints index